Snowboarding

by Gail Blasser Riley

COVER-TO-COVER BOOKS

Book Design: Mark Hagenberg
Photo Research: Lisa Lorimor

While many of the photos feature snowboarders not wearing helmets, the author and publisher do not endorse participation in the sport without helmets and recommend the use of helmets for safe and enjoyable snowboarding.

Image Credits:
Associated Press: pp. 7, 10, 12, 14–15, 23, 24, 25, 26, 27, 28; Toyadz: p. 18; Wild Mountain: p. 40

Corel: pp. 11, 20, 50; Photos.com: cover, pp. 1, 3, 5, 6, 8, 13, 16, 17, 21, 22, 29, 30, 31, 33, 34, 35, 36, 37, 39, 42, 43, 44, 45, 47, 48, 49, 51, 52, 53, 54, 55, 56, 58–59, 60–61, 62–63 Royalty-Free/CORBIS: p. 46

Perfection Learning® Corporation
1000 North Second Avenue, P. O. Box 500, Logan, Iowa 51546-0500.
Tel: 1-800-831-4190 • Fax: 1-800-543-2745
perfectionlearning.com

1   2   3   4   5   6   PP   09   08   07   06   05   04

Paperback ISBN 0-7891-6414-0
Cover Craft® ISBN 0-7569-3176-2

Contents
Snowboarding

History

of Snowboarding

1929 M. J. Burchett uses clothesline and horse reins to tie his feet to a plywood board.

1963 Tom Sims constructs what he calls the Ski-Board.

1965 Sherman Poppen invents the Snurfer.

1970 Dimitrije Milovich begins a limited production of **custom** snowboards with metal edges.

1975 Milovich creates Winterstick, a snowboard-production company.

1977 Jake Burton Carpenter starts his snowboard, accessory, and apparel company—Burton Snowboards. His company still leads the industry today.

1979 Production of the Snurfer ends.

The first **halfpipe** is discovered in Tahoe City, California.

1981 Modern competitive snowboarding begins with a small contest held in April at Ski Cooper in Leadville, Colorado.

1982 First National Snowsurfing Championship competition is held at Suicide Six Ski Area in Woodstock, Vermont.

1983 First World Snowboarding Championships are held near Lake Tahoe, Nevada. The first halfpipe event is held here.

1985 Only seven percent of the U.S. ski areas allow snowboarding.

The first snowboarding magazine, *Absolutely Radical*, is published. Six months later its name is changed to *International Snowboard Magazine*.

Snowboarding Today

Today 97 percent of U.S. resort areas welcome snowboarders. It has been predicted that by 2012 snowboarders will outnumber skiers.

1986 Stratton Mountain in Vermont becomes the first resort to offer organized snowboarding instruction.

1987 The first World Cup is held with two events in both Europe and the United States.

1988 The U.S. **Amateur** Snowboarding Association (USASA) is formed as the first governing body for competitive amateur snowboarding.

1989 Most of the major ski resorts (such as Squaw Valley, California; Vail, Colorado; Sun Valley, Idaho; and Snowbird, Utah) open their slopes to snowboarders.

1990 Vail creates a snowboard park.

The International Snowboarding Federation (ISF) is founded and becomes a ruling body for international snowboarding competition.

1994 *The Wall Street Journal* proclaims, "Snowboarding scores as the fastest growing sport with participation up 50 percent since the previous winter."

1995 The International Olympic Committee declares that snowboarding will be a medal event in the 1998 Games.

1998 For the first time, snowboarding events are included in the Olympic Games in Nagano, Japan. The United States wins two bronze medals.

2002 U.S. Olympic snowboarder Kelly Clark wins the gold medal in the women's halfpipe competition. Americans Ross Powers, Danny Kass, and J. J. Thomas sweep the men's halfpipe event.

The International Snowboarding Federation folds after experiencing financial difficulties. It can no longer compete with the International Ski Federation, which the International Olympic Committee recognizes as the governing body for snowboarding.

Chapter 1

Action!

On the Hill

It was February 2002. Puffs of breath filled the icy air. Bells rang out. Reporters chatted into microphones. People in bright coats and jackets dotted the snowy hills like a colorful carpet. Photographers snapped endless photos, and video cameras rolled.

Nervous riders waited to take to the white blanket of snow. Olympic victory was just around the corner for someone.

The entire world waited to see what would happen as the riders sped into the halfpipe. Who would take home Olympic gold, silver, and bronze medals?

American Kelly Clark prepared mentally for her **run**. She saw the halfpipe stretching out ahead of her. The seconds ticked by.

Kelly Clark

The Competition

Clark's competitors included fellow Americans Tricia Byrnes and Shannon Dunn.

Byrnes had made a disappointing first run. She opened with huge **straight airs**. Unfortunately, the strength of the run hadn't held. When Byrnes tried her **McTwist**, she crashed into the halfpipe without completing the move.

This didn't break Byrnes' spirit. In her second run, she made a fine showing with the McTwist. She placed sixth.

What about Shannon Dunn? What were her chances of winning a medal in the Games? Dunn had won a bronze medal at the Nagano, Japan, Olympic Games four years earlier.

Dunn's previous run in the 2002 Salt Lake City Olympic Games had been a good effort, but it wasn't good enough. She did not place in the top three. Dunn's first run had included a McTwist and a **720** near the beginning. Her second run included a huge **method**. She followed with a solid McTwist. To wind up, she hit a **crippler** 720 with a **grab**, and she **stuck** the landing!

No other woman had even attempted a crippler 720. Even with Dunn's fine showing, the judges only placed her fifth. Dunn knew that she wouldn't win a medal. But there was still a chance for the United States—Kelly Clark.

Other key competitors included the current world champion, Doriane Vidal of France, and Fabienne Reuteler of Switzerland. Both were right up there at the top. Vidal was currently first. Reuteler was right behind.

Vidal had made a fine showing. She had landed a **frontside** 720 and solid straight-air grabs.

Reuteler had pounded out a **backside 540** and a 720. Both Vidal and Reuteler had completed outstanding runs. But had they been strong enough to take the two top slots? Only Clark's run could answer that question.

Clark's Run

Clark knew one thing for certain as she stared down at the halfpipe. She needed a score of 43 to take home the gold.

How Competition Is Judged

Olympic halfpipe competition is judged by five judges. Each judge scores one **aspect** of a competitor's run.

Judge 1: Straight airs (looking at style)

Judge 2: Rotations (looking at spins over 360 degrees)

Judge 3: Amplitude (looking at how high the trick is above the pipe)

Judges 4 and 5: Overall impression (looking for difficulty, risks taken, and how the run is put together overall)

Each judge can award up to 10 points. The points of the five judges are added together to come up with the final score. A score of 50 points is possible.

Clark eyed the halfpipe. She was off in a shot, racing into the **powder**. She soared to new heights with gigantic straight-air grabs. She charted an early **lien** 540. She ended her run with a huge McTwist-to-720 combo—an awesome run!

As she sailed out of the halfpipe, she must have wondered if the run had been good enough. Had it been solid enough to take gold? The minutes must have ticked away like hours as Clark waited.

Fabienne Reuteler, Kelly Clark, and Doriane Vidal at the 2002 Olympics

The Score

Clark wasn't the only one who waited for the judges' decision. Her team members waited. Doriane Vidal and Fabienne Reuteler waited. Reporters waited. The crowd waited. People all over the globe, who were watching the event on television, waited. Had the run been good enough? Would Clark take gold?

47. 9! Clark scored well above the 43 she needed to take home the medal.

Later, on the awards platform, the U. S. flag flew in the top spot as the U. S. national anthem filled the air. Doriane Vidal took silver, and Fabienne Reuteler took the bronze home to Switzerland.

Chapter 2

Snowboarding
for Everyone

Snowboarding action comes in many packages. What's your style? Which kind of snowboarding is your favorite? Do you lean toward **alpine boarding**? Do you glide through **freeride**? Perhaps **freestyle** is more to your liking. A snowboarder's preference will influence almost everything about the snowboarding experience—from the board to the slope.

Alpine Boarding

Alpine racers zip through competitions such as the giant **slalom**. Who is the winner? It's the racer who sails through all the **gates** in the fastest time.

Competitors are not permitted to take practice runs on alpine courses. But they are allowed to walk or **sideslip** through the course. When riders sideslip, they glide slowly through the course on their boards. As they do, the competitors note everything about the course, such as where the gates are and the condition of the course.

French snowboarder Mathieu Bozzetto at a racing event in Canada

Freeriding

What if competition is not at the top of your list? You're not interested in judges and scores. You'd rather take a more **laid-back** approach to riding. Then freeriding is for you. This style more closely resembles downhill skiing.

Many snowboarders enjoy the freedom and creativity of freeriding. This style adapts to any **terrain**. It's also called *all-mountain riding* since riding the terrain often requires the rider to use jumps and turns. It's a "do-your-own-thing" style of snowboarding.

Most beginners start with freeriding. This is the style used on most ski slopes.

Freestyle

Freestyle is considered the most spectacular style of snowboarding. It involves riding a halfpipe and performing tricks high in the air. The tricks are usually in the form of twists, turns, grabs, and other extreme **aerial** movements.

Halfpipe riding is not about speed. When snowboarders are in a speed race, the winner is **indisputable**. It's the racer who follows all the rules in the fastest time. Halfpipe competitors are judged on their tricks. The judges' scores are often questioned because they are partially based on opinion.

THE HALFPIPE

If you're a skateboarder, you probably already know about the halfpipe. Riders were skateboarding through halfpipes before they snowboarded through them. You'll see many of the same tricks used by snowboarders and skateboarders.

The First Halfpipe

In 1979, Mark Anolik stumbled onto the Tahoe City Halfpipe. He was boarding around the Tahoe City, California, dump when he found this natural snow halfpipe. It was the first snowboarding halfpipe. The pipe attracted snowboarders and photographers from across the United States.

Today's snowboarding halfpipes are carved out of the snow by special machines. What does a halfpipe look like, and what are its parts?

A halfpipe is a U-shaped bowl. Riders move from wall to wall making jumps and performing tricks.

On top of each side of a halfpipe is a flat part, or the deck. At the edge of the deck is the lip. The entry ramp is the part of the deck where riders **drop in** and begin their runs.

The inside bottom of the pipe is the flat. The walls slope up from the bottom on both sides of the flat to the deck.

Shaun White performs at the 2002 Winter Olympics in Utah

Wall

Flat

Lip

Deck

Riders do all sorts of tricks on the halfpipe walls. Each wall has two parts—the transition

Now That's High!

The walls in the Salt Lake City Olympic Games were 15 feet high. During the men's competition, Ross Powers earned his gold in part by flying 15 feet above the pipe. That's 30 feet above the ground!

and the vertical. The transitions, or trannies, are the curved parts of the walls between the horizontal flat and the vertical walls. The verticals, or verts, are the sections of the walls between the lip and the transitions.

Vertical

Transition

Horizontal

Chapter 3

Back to the Past

Putting the Board Before the Sport

By 2000, more than 7 million people were snowboarding! How did this sport become so popular? Where did it start?

M. J. BURCHETT

Some people trace the roots of snowboarding back to 1929. M. J. Burchett wanted to stand up as he glided down a snowy hill. So he used clothesline and horse reins to tie his feet to a plywood board. Burchett's sport didn't catch on. Many years passed before more pages were added to snowboarding history.

SHERMAN POPPEN

In 1965, Sherman Poppen, a chemical engineer from Michigan, watched his daughter slide down a hill while standing on her sled. As he watched, he came up with a great idea. He bolted together a pair of children's snow skis. Then he attached a rope to the front of the "board." His daughter could hold the rope and ski/surf her way down the hill.

Poppen's wife is credited for coming up with the name. Just as her husband had put the skis together, she put the two words *snow* and *surf* together to form the name of the board—Snurfer.

Over the next few years, more than a million Snurfers were sold in toy stores and sporting goods stores for about $10–$15 each. Poppen even arranged competitions for Snurfer riders.

People used Snurfers to ride down snowy hills. But the boards didn't have bindings to hold boots to the boards. So riders' feet would slip and slide on the boards. Several riders realized the Snurfer needed improvements.

DIMITRIJE MILOVICH

In 1970, surfer Dimitrije Milovich tried sliding down snowy hills on cafeteria trays. This gave him the idea for his snowboard. He used ideas from skis and surfboards to come up with his snowboard design—the Winterstick.

Milovich opened his snowboard company in 1975. His work and designs helped to make snowboarding a widely known sport. Many major magazines published articles about his snowboards.

JAKE BURTON CARPENTER

Another important snowboard creator was Jake Burton Carpenter. He wanted a surfboard, but his parents refused. So Carpenter hopped aboard a Snurfer when he was 14. He rode in some of Poppen's competitions.

By 1977, Carpenter had made improvements to his Snurfer and created his own snowboard design with bindings. He created a company, Burton Snowboards, to build custom boards for other people.

After two years, Carpenter was over $100,000 in debt. He was discouraged, but he kept hoping the sport would catch on.

Putting the Sport Before the Board

Jake Burton Carpenter realized that before his company could be successful, the market for snowboards had to broaden. He shifted his focus to the sport of snowboarding, not the product. He began promoting the sport instead of his product. His first catalogs introduced the sport first without even mentioning Burton boards. He organized snowboarding events that brought national attention to the sport. Carpenter also became a driving force in convincing resorts to accept snowboarding.

As a result, Burton Snowboards has become one of the best-known and most successful snowboard companies in the world.

Snowboarders Allowed

By the middle of the 1980s, snowboarders had taken to the ski slopes. By the late 1980s, most resorts began to allow snowboarders to ride down the slopes alongside skiers.

Resorts began to recognize that snowboarding had come to stay. In 1990, Vail Resort created a snowboard park as part of its landscape.

Chapter 4

Let the
Competition Begin!

The year was 1982. The place was snowy Woodstock, Vermont. Sports broadcasters and writers gathered in the icy cold. They set up their cameras or prepared to write. Chills and thrills filled the air.

Snowboarders' breath filtered out in puffs as they made their way to the top of the slope. They prepared for slalom and downhill races.

This was the scene of a first and a last. It was the first National Snowsurfing Championship competition. It was the last time snowboards and Snurfers took to the powder in the same competition.

More Snowboards— More Competitions

There was another first in 1982. Chris Sanders and Earl Zellers began a new company, Avalanche Snowboards. They produced three types of snowboards. The boards' names were just as creative as the boards themselves—Huey, Dewey, and Louie.

In the spring of 1983, Jake Burton Carpenter hosted the National Snowboarding Championships at Snow Valley in Vermont as a way to promote the sport.

Other competitions began that year as well. At the Soda Springs Ski Bowl near Lake Tahoe, the first halfpipe event was held.

Snowboarding continued to grow as more and more competitions introduced the sport around the world. In 1990, the International Snowboarding Federation (ISF) was created as a ruling body for international snowboarding competition.

Read All About It!

In 1985, a snowboarding magazine appeared on the scene. It was called *Absolutely Radical*. Its name later changed to *International Snowboard Magazine*. For the first time ever, a major magazine covered only the sport of snowboarding. In the past, the sport had been covered by magazines such as *Thrasher*, a skateboarding magazine.

Going for the Gold

Snowboarding had soared to great heights by 1998. For the first time, Olympic hopefuls took to the slopes in Nagano, Japan. Events included halfpipe and giant slalom for women and men. The United States took home two bronze medals—Ross Powers for the men's halfpipe and Shannon Dunn for the women's halfpipe.

What happened during the next Olympic Games was a complete surprise. In the 2002 Salt Lake City Olympic Games, Kelly Clark of the United States took gold in the women's halfpipe competition.

Ross Powers, Danny Kass, and J. J. Thomas proved to be a triple threat in the 2002 Olympic Games. They gave the United States a medal sweep. It was the first medal sweep in one event for the United States in 46 years!

Danny Kass, Ross Powers, and J. J. Thomas at the 2002 Winter Olympics in Utah

Chapter 5

The Greats

Kelly Clark

You read about Kelly Clark's gold medal run in the first chapter. But did you know that in 1985 Clark was just two years old when she first took to the ski slopes in Vermont? She didn't think skiing was fun. So she started snowboarding in third grade.

When Clark was 13, she began entering competitions. She continued to develop skill in her sport.

In 2003, Clark took second place in the halfpipe event in the Winter X Games held in Aspen, Colorado. Today she is a member of the Burton Global Team, sponsored by Burton Snowboards.

Clark also enjoys surfing and playing tennis. It will be hard for anything to top the gold medal run she had in 2002!

Kelly Clark

Keir Dillon

Keir Dillon

Keir Dillon was born in Pennsylvania in 1977. "My dad was a real ski dog," Keir once said. "So he had me out on skis early. I learned when I was about four or five years old."

Dillon began boarding when he was 12. Three years later, he was entering competitions. He really became serious about riding after his first year of college.

Today he has won medals in **boardercross** and freestyle contests. He finished in the top ten in halfpipe at the 1999 World Snowboarding Championships. And he finished second in a Tokyo competition, winning a prize of $10,000! But his crowning achievement was being named to the U. S. snowboard team for the 2002 Olympics.

Shannon Dunn

Shannon Dunn

Taking home an Olympic medal—
what a thrill! Shannon Dunn took home
the bronze from the 1998 Nagano, Japan,
Games. Her love for the snow began in
1975 when she was just three years old.
It was the beginning of her skiing and
snowboarding career.

Dunn started boarding on a rental
board when she was 16. From the first
time she stepped on a board, she was
hooked. But it was hard for her to find a
resort that would allow snowboarding.

Dunn is often considered a pioneer
in women's snowboarding. She once told
ESPN, "When I first learned to ride, my
friend Betsy and I were some of the first
girls on my mountain. . . . We just did it
because it was fun. We didn't think it
was a big deal that we were some of the
only girls. I just did my own thing. Then
the next thing I know, time has flown by,
and I am a pioneer in the sport."

Ross Powers

Ross Powers

Ross Powers was born in 1979. He was only a toddler when he first took to the slopes on skis. He was six when a friend gave him one of the first Burton snowboards.

Powers lived on his board. He spent every weekend perfecting his skills. He raced for the slopes as soon as school was out each day.

Powers entered a halfpipe competition during his first year in high school. He didn't expect much. He had always concentrated on racing. He surprised himself by winning.

Then Powers accepted an invitation to join the U. S. snowboard team. At first, Powers made an effort to compete in freestyle and racing. He soon learned that practice just took too much time for him to be his best in both. His focus turned entirely to the halfpipe.

Powers' gold-medal run was unforgettable. He jumped and soared 15 feet above the pipe. He rode parallel to the ground! The sun outlined his profile in the glistening snow below.

Then Powers made two spins. He did a somersault during one! Other tricks included a switch McTwist, a **mute grab**, and a **stalefish**. He stuck every landing.

After he won the gold, Powers said, "I couldn't ask for anything more."

Shaun White

Shaun White was born in San Diego, California, in 1986. At 16, he was considered one of the best **professional** snowboarders in the world. He was known as one of the most talented halfpipe riders in recent memory. He won every major competition he entered in 2003, including the Winter X Games. White is one of the most respected and dominant riders in the sport today. He is ranked first in the world.

Besides being a professional snowboarder, White competes as a pro skateboarder. He once told an interviewer, "Both of the sports influence each other. I take a lot of tricks from snowboarding into skateboarding and vice versa."

Fabienne Reuteler

Fabienne Reuteler was born in 1979 in Switzerland. The 2000–2001 season was her first as a pro. By the end of the season, she had placed third in the Winter X Games and was ranked second in the world in the halfpipe.

In addition to boarding, Reuteler found time to graduate from the University of Hagen in Germany with a degree in economics. She speaks four languages—German, English, French, and Italian.

In a recent interview, Reuteler said, "I like to go fast. Besides pipe riding, I like to go freeriding and take jumps. That all makes you confident in the pipe."

Fabienne Reuteler

Chapter 6

The Essentials

Before you can snowboard, you will need some very important pieces of equipment.

Boards

What kind of board should you buy? This depends on the type of snowboarding you plan to do.

The freestyle board is short and wide. This makes it a strong board for doing tricks in the air. This is the type of board a snowboarder would use to ride a halfpipe.

The freeride board is a good choice for beginning snowboarders. It's the easiest board to ride on or off a trail.

The race, or alpine, boards are used by riders who plan to compete in slalom and other downhill races. These boards move quickly and turn well.

Choosing the type of board is only one step. The size of the board is also important. How does a rider choose the best size? If a rider is planning to race, a longer board is usually a better choice. For tricks, the shorter board works better.

Suppose a rider is new to snowboarding. A shorter board would be the better choice since it's easier to control.

Riders should learn all they can about the different boards before they go shopping.

PARTS OF THE BOARD

Think of a board's nose as its front and its tail as the back. Sometimes, it can be difficult to tell which end is the nose on freeride and freestyle boards. An alpine board's tip is often more pointed than its tail. Ask the salesperson to help you if you can't tell which end is the front.

The base is the bottom of the board that slides on the snow, and the deck is the part of the board where the bindings are found. The toe edge is the side the toes point to. And the heel edge is near the heels.

The stomp pad is the nonskid rubber mat next to the back-foot binding. This is where the back foot rests when it is out of the binding. It is used when entering, riding, and exiting a **chairlift**.

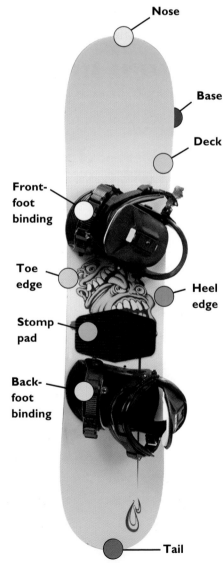

Nose

Base

Deck

Front-foot binding

Toe edge

Heel edge

Stomp pad

Back-foot binding

Tail

Bindings and Boots

Bindings hold the boots to the snowboard. Four major types of bindings are available—highback/strap, step-in, Flow In, and plate. Many riders like the convenience of the step-in bindings. But others think the strap bindings are more comfortable. The binding choice also depends on the riding style and the type of boot worn.

STRAP BINDINGS

Many riders prefer the strap binding. Usually, strap binding is less expensive. The high back plate and the front strap gives a rider more control over the board. The soft boots that are worn with the strap-in bindings are more comfortable. One drawback of these bindings is that the straps often need to be adjusted and readjusted.

STEP-IN BINDINGS

A step-in binding comes with a stiffer boot. Some riders prefer these bindings and boots because of the convenience. But many riders don't like the stiffer boots and bindings. They don't bend as easily, which causes problems with control.

FLOW IN SYSTEM

Recently the Flow In system was introduced. These bindings use soft boots, and have the high back of strap bindings and the convenience of step-in bindings. One disadvantage is that the Flow In bindings are not as easy to adjust as strap bindings. Still, these bindings are growing in popularity.

PLATE BINDINGS

Plate bindings consist of a hard base plate and steel **bails** that hold hard boots in the bindings. Alpine racers like these bindings because the racers have better control on sharp, downhill turns at high speeds.

Keeping You Warm and Dry—Clothing

The clothing you choose for snowboarding is very important. Remember, your clothes will become wet. Think about the fabric. Does it provide good protection against the wet snow and from the biting wind and cold?

Think layers! Go for big! Each piece of clothing must be large enough to fit comfortably over the pieces below it. Layering your clothing will keep you warm on the cold days. It will allow you to shed a layer on the warmer days.

BASE LAYER

Depending on the temperature, a snowboarder's first layer of clothing is thermal underwear. The shirt and pants are made of lightweight material that keeps the rider warm and dry by transferring moisture to the next layer.

Snowboarding socks are a must. The specially designed socks have extra insulation in the soles to keep a rider's feet warm. The socks have extra cushion to protect feet from hard **impacts**.

Second Layer

The second layer consists of a fleece or wool sweater and snowboard pants. The sweater and pants should be made of materials that allow the rider freedom of movement.

Snowboarding boots finish off the layer. They should work together with the snowboard bindings to keep the rider's body connected to the snowboard.

Third Layer

A jacket should keep the snowboarder warm and dry. More expensive jackets usually have waterproofing that doesn't wear off as the jacket grows older. They also have good venting. This allows perspiration to vent out through the jacket, keeping the rider dry.

Some riders look for jackets with a hood. Others want all sorts of "bells and whistles," such as pockets everywhere, striking colors and designs, or fancy zippers. These are just matters of personal preference.

It's very important for riders to keep their hands warm. Snowboarders choose between gloves and mittens. Many believe that mittens are a better choice for warmth. Hands tend to stay warmer in mittens because the fingers are all together. Most gloves and mittens are padded to protect the hands from impacts with the ground.

Keeping You Safe—Safety Gear

HELMET

Choose a helmet that is comfortable and fits well. The helmet is the most important part of a snowboarder's safety equipment. Wearing a helmet drastically reduces head injury during a fall or other impact. Helmets should carry a CE, ASTM, or Snell RS-98 certification.

This means that the helmet model has undergone a battery of tests to determine its performance during an accident.

GOGGLES

Goggles offer protection from the sun and ultraviolet rays. The sun is brighter at high altitudes and when it reflects off snow. The UV rays can damage your eyes and cause snow blindness.

Goggles also prevent snow and ice particles from falling into a rider's eyes. They keep twigs from hitting riders' faces when riders go off trail or into the backcountry and board through the trees.

Always try on the goggles with the helmet. This is the only way to know whether the fit is right.

Lens Colors

Lenses for goggles come in many colors that are specific for different conditions.

- Black lenses reduce glare without changing colors. They are suitable for bright, sunny conditions.
- Green or silver lenses are suitable for most bright conditions.
- Yellow, amber, or gold lenses filter out blue light and bring out shadows, making the goggles suitable for most conditions and especially in low to moderate light.
- Purple or rose lenses are best used in low-light conditions.
- Clear goggles are usually the best choice for night, dusk, or very cloudy conditions.

LEASH

During a fall or improper move, a rider sometimes loses the board, and it slides away. It could sail into another person and cause an injury. This can be prevented.

A snowboard leash is a cord or strap that links the rider's front leg to the front binding on the snowboard. Some snowboard leashes are very small hooks that loop around the binding and clip to a key ring on the rider's bootlaces.

Chapter 7

Safety First

Safety is important for all snowboarders. These are some of the more common injuries and how to prevent them.

Wrist Injuries

Wrist injuries are common, especially when someone is just learning how to ride. New riders often fall, catching themselves with their hands. Sprains and fractures can occur. Separate wrist guards can be purchased. Some mittens and gloves have wrist guards built into them. Riders should train themselves not to fall with their hands flat to the ground. Instead they should form fists and try to land on their forearms. The forearms are stronger and can take more shock, thus reducing the chance of serious injury.

Knee Injuries

Knees act like springs or shock absorbers for the body. Most knee injuries are caused by very hard impacts or impacts from unexpected turning motions. As their technique improves, riders are able to handle harder impacts. Riders must keep their knees bent at all times during snowboarding, especially during tricks and jumps. Locking the knees takes the spring out of the legs.

Ankle Injuries

Ankle injuries usually occur during failed jumps or crashes. Soft boots are preferred by boarders even though wearing them increases the chances of ankle injuries. People with weak ankles should choose harder boots.

Other Injuries

Many injuries are caused by snowboarders crashing into other objects or people. When boarding on busy slopes, the chances of hitting another boarder or skier increases. Every boarder and skier should follow the skier and snowboarder's Responsibility Code.

The Responsibility Code

1. Be sure you have enough control of your board to stop or avoid objects when needed. You can push your boundaries, but know your limit.
2. People ahead of you have the right-of-way. It is your responsibility to avoid hitting slower boarders or skiers.
3. Do not stop, sit down, or rest on a trail. If you do, make sure you are out of the general traffic path and that other people can see you clearly.
4. When you start your run, check around you before entering the trail.
5. Use a leash or other device that will prevent your board from sliding down the slope and possibly hitting someone should you lose control.
6. Follow the resort or park rules. Follow all signs and do not go onto closed trails or into restricted areas.
7. Check the weather, snow conditions, and routes in the area where you are planning to board. Do not take chances if the weather or other conditions are unfavorable.
8. Do not make jumps if you cannot see the landing site. Never ride hard into an unknown area.
9. If you are involved in an accident, stay on the scene. Offer assistance to the injured. Report the accident to the patrol of the resort or the party in charge of the area.
10. Never go off trail alone. Stay in close contact with the people you are going off trail with.
11. Learn how to ride a chairlift safely before attempting to use one.

This is only part of the code that is officially endorsed by the National Ski Areas Association, the National Ski Patrol, and the Professional Ski Instructors of America.

Avoiding Injuries

To lessen the chances of injury, riders should do some warm-up and stretching exercises. Exercise steps up blood flow, which warms muscles and lubricates joints. Do exercises that concentrate on the muscles you will be using most—lower and upper legs, buttocks, back, and neck. The exercises can be as simple as walking up and down the slope, sidestepping, and jumping.

Chapter 8

Maps, Signs, and Markers

Trail maps are filled with markers and signs that give snowboarders and skiers important information. What can you learn from a trail map? You can locate trails, lodges, restaurants, first aid stations, and chairlifts. More importantly, you can choose a trail that fits your experience.

SKI/SNOWBOARD AREA TRAIL MAP

Expect the Unexpected — Trail and slope conditions vary constantly with weather conditions and skier use. Be aware of changing conditions, natural or man made.

Wild Mountain

How Difficult?

Signs and markers along a trail tell the difficulty level of the run. The difficulty markers are international. The same symbols are used on trails around the world. Skiers and snowboarders will know how difficult a trail is even if they can't speak or read the language in the country they're visiting.

A green circle shows you the easiest trails. These are good spots for a beginners.

A blue square indicates an easy-to-intermediate trail. This is the type of trail to try after you've had quite a bit of experience in snowboarding. It's not a spot for beginners.

One diamond marks an advanced trail—one that is difficult.

Two diamonds tell you that a trail is very difficult. Only the most experienced snowboarders should try these trails.

Signs of Difficulty

Easy

Intermediate

Advanced

Very Advanced

Here's something to keep in mind even if you've already been snowboarding for a while. The difficulty markers only compare the level of difficulty on the mountain where they are located. Suppose that you've been snowboarding in Pennsylvania. Then you visit the slopes in Colorado. An intermediate trail on the Colorado slope could be much more difficult than an intermediate trail on the Pennsylvania slope.

Also, a trail's difficulty level can change with the weather. Icy weather makes trails slippery. Windy weather can blow so much snow across a trail that it becomes difficult to even see where the trail is.

What other signs might you see on a trail? You might see a marker with the word *slow*. It's important to slow down when you see one of these signs. Often, this will tell you that you're coming to a very busy area, and you don't want to run into anybody!

You also might see a sign with a plus sign. This sign indicates that a first aid station is nearby.

Warning! Danger!

Anytime you see yellow markers, be sure to give them close attention. They tell you that danger lies ahead. Most often these yellow caution signs have a red triangle surrounding a red exclamation mark. Words are written below explaining the danger.

What if you see a marker with an X inside a triangle? This means that two trails or a trail and a chairlift cross paths. It's important to watch out for riders who might be in your way.

How Do You Get There from Here?

Not all signs and markers tell you about safety. Some just tell you how to find where you're going. For example, some signs show you how to reach a nearby chairlift. Look for a symbol of people sitting on a chairlift.

Do you know the name of the trail you're looking for? Perhaps you're looking for the simplest way to move down a trail. Maybe you're looking for a ski lodge. Signs and arrows can point you in the right direction.

• • • •

Before starting on a trail, it's important to understand what all the signs mean. Be sure to ask someone in charge if you need more information.

Regular stance

Chapter 9

Got Moves?

First Things First

Are you a regular or a goofy foot? No, this doesn't have anything to do with how silly you are. It has to do with the way you stand on the board. This is your **stance**. Do you ride with the right foot forward? If so, you ride goofy. If your left foot is forward, you ride regular. About 80 percent of riders have a regular stance.

Goofy Foot

This name was given to the stance because the Disney character Goofy rode a skateboard with the right foot forward in an old Disney cartoon.

44

How do you figure out whether you ride goofy or regular? Are you a surfer? Do you skateboard? If so, you'll probably place the same foot forward on a snowboard. If you don't know, try running and sliding across a smooth surface. Which foot do you put in front as you begin to slide? This is the foot you will put up front on the board.

Walking and the Other First Steps

Before the tricks and before the racing, you must learn the first steps in snowboarding. Then you will be ready for a simple glide down a very short, easy slope—the **bunny slope**. Beginning riders should try each one of these moves until they are comfortable. These moves create the basis for all the others.

SIDESLIPPING

Sideslipping is a controlled downhill slide along the fall line. First, you need to figure out where the fall line is. This isn't a real line. It's the route that something rolling down the slope would follow or the direction that gravity pulls you.

To sideslip, put your board across the fall line. Control the board by rolling it off and onto its edges. This will help you learn to control your balance. Rolling the board on the edges stops or slows the board's slide, much like a car brake would. Practice sideslipping until you are able to accelerate and slow down at will, using both the toe and heel edges.

GLIDING

When gliding, it's important to remember to stay balanced over your front foot. Begin by practicing on a gentle, short slope. Point your board down the fall line. Shift your weight over your front foot until you begin to glide. Keep your arms and head up and face forward.

TURNING

Good snowboarders make turns look easy. But it takes practice to make them. After your coach or an experienced rider shows you how to make a turn, take plenty of time to practice. Be sure to practice both toe-side and heel-side turns. Before you know it, you'll be turning one turn after another!

Toe-side turn

Tail grab

Expert Freestyle Moves

There are many freestyle moves.
Many of them reflect skateboarding
moves. It's best to have an instructor
or an experienced boarder show
how the moves are done.

GRAB

Go into the air and grab the
board with your hand. Each grab has
a different name depending on where
and with which hand the board is
grabbed. Some favorite grabs include
the method, the iguana, the stalefish,
the melancholy, and the double.

Method grab

Indy grab

Nose bone

NOSE BONES AND TAILBONES

Jump into the air and straighten out one or both legs. You've done a bone. Did you straighten your back leg? You've done a tailbone. Did you straighten your front leg? That's a nose bone. Some riders also call this *poking*.

OLLIE

Want to jump into the air? Then it's time for an ollie! As you ride, bend your knees just a bit. Jump! As you jump, bring up your front foot. Feel the air? Now pull your knees toward your chest. Sail to the ground and stick your landing!

SHIFTIE

Take off in a jump. Twist your upper body in one direction. Twist your lower body in the other. You've just done a shiftie! Just before you come down, shift your body back so you can stick the landing.

Shiftie

Sidekick

SIDEKICK

Jump! Pull up your feet as if you're about to kick yourself in the rear. You've just done a sidekick.

SPIN

Ready for a complete spin? Then you're ready for a 360 air, or a 3! You'll want to begin your spin just as soon as you're into the jump. Your upper body should stay low as you turn one complete revolution. Stick your landing! Once you've learned to spin, you can add revolutions. These spins are often just referred to as a 5 (540 or one and a half revolutions), a 7 (720 or two complete revolutions), and a 9 (900 or two and a half revolutions).

After you've learned the basic moves, you can begin combining them just as the pros do.

Chapter 10

And the Word Is...

As in any sport, snowboarding has a language all its own. Here are some of the terms you're likely to find as you learn more about snowboarding.

air dog boarder who jumps most of the time and is most interested in aerial tricks

bail to crash; to fall

beat used to describe something that is not good

boardhead name for someone who snowboards

bonk to hit something with your snowboard

boost to catch air from a jump or a halfpipe

chatter unnecessary vibration in a board that happens at higher speeds and through turns, making the board harder to control

corduroy used to describe a freshly groomed trail because it has a finely ridged surface

cruiser run relaxed run on a fairly smooth trail

duck foot standing with your toes pointing outward

effective edge part of the board that touches the snow

face plant used to describe a face-first fall

fakie riding backward

flail to ride badly and out of control

flatland used to describe tricks performed on a flat trail with obstacles

glide to slide through the snow without using the edges of the snowboard

grommet *or* grom name for a small, young snowboarder

hardpack snow that is very firm

head wall place where a road cuts across a trail and creates a flat spot on the hill, making it a good place to catch air

hit each time a rider goes into the air and performs a trick

hucker person who travels crazily into the air and does not land on his or her feet

jam session halfpipe competition where all competitors ride the halfpipe continuously during one allotted amount of time. Judges watch the jam session and choose the best riders.

jibber person who rides like a skateboarder doing lots of tricks on things other than snow, such as rails, trees, garbage cans, or logs

lame used to describe something that is not good

late move added to a trick just before the landing

mogul big bump in the snow

pack to fall or crash

phat used to describe something exceptional

pipe dragon machine that shapes the walls of a halfpipe

poser someone who pretends to be something he or she is
not

powder dry, light, deep snow that is preferred by boarders

rolling down the windows used to describe someone who
is caught off balance and is rotating his or her arms wildly in
the air to try to recover

session certain interval of time in which someone snowboards

shredding doing some fine riding

sick used to describe something really good

skating pushing the board with your back foot on the ground
while the other foot is in the binding

sketching riding unsteadily and nearly falling. Judges will take
away points for sketchy riding.

slopestyle competition a competition in which boarders
ride over a series of various kinds of jumps and are judged
on the tricks and maneuvers

snake used to describe someone who cuts in front of
someone else

snow cat machine that smooths out the snow and prepares a
slope for skiers and snowboarders

speed check riding sideways to slow down

stoked psyched; excited

stomp to make a good landing

tight wonderful; terrific

traverse to ride across a hill

tucking jumping with your knees pulled toward your chest

wack something that is not good

wipeout big fall

yard sale used to describe a scattering of
equipment over the trail from
a fall

Chapter 11

Snowboarding Organizations and Web Sites

Want to find out more about snowboarding? Perhaps you'd like to find out about competition. What are the rules? Who makes the rules? How are the rules enforced? Where are the competitions held? How do you compete? Who are the major riders? Check out these snowboarding organizations and Web sites.

United States of America Snowboard Association (USASA)

United States of America Snowboard Association
Post Office Box 624262
South Lake Tahoe, CA 96154
www.usasa.org

The USASA is a national association for snowboard competitors. It sets up competition rules and events.

National Ski Patrol (NSP)

www.nsp.org

This Web site provides a great deal of useful information and links, including current weather conditions, winter safety information, how to avoid injury, and how to choose snowboard equipment. The site also provides links to snowboarding discussion boards.

United States Ski and Snowboard Association

United States Ski and Snowboard
  Association
1500 Kearns Boulevard
Park City, UT 84060

www.ussa.org

This site provides information about the U. S. team, including competitions and team members.

Glossary

aerial   in the air

alpine boarding   snowboarding that focuses on making sharp, hard turns while speeding downhill

amateur   relating to someone who does something just for the pleasure of doing it

aspect   part

backside   referring to the heelside wall, or the wall the rider's back faces

bail   hinged bar on a binding that comes up over the toe of the boot to hold the boot to the board

boardercross   competition in which snowboarders race head-to-head over an obstacle course containing various jumps and banked turns

bunny slope   gentlest slope at a ski resort, which is designed for beginners

chairlift	motorized suspended chair system that takes riders from the bottom of a mountain to the top
crippler	trick in which the snowboarder rides forward, does a flip, and ends forward. The number of revolutions may vary.
custom	built to order
drop in	enter a halfpipe (see separate glossary entry) from the top by dropping over the edge and landing on the board
540	spin consisting of one and a half revolutions
freeride	laid-back (see separate glossary entry) snowboarding that allows the boarder to ride, turn, and jump over any terrain (see separate glossary entry)
freestyle	snowboarding that involves doing tricks in the air in snowboard parks, halfpipes (see separate glossary entry), and natural obstacles found on mountains

frontside	referring to the toeside wall, or the wall the rider is facing
gate	space between two markers through which a boarder passes in a slalom (see separate glossary entry) race
grab	move that includes gripping the edge of the board with one or both hands
halfpipe	large frozen snow structure in the shape of the bottom half of a pipe used for freestyle (see separate glossary entry) snowboarding
impact	force with which one object hits another
indisputable	not open to argument
laid-back	relaxed
lien	trick in which the front hand grabs the heel edge and the body leans out over the nose
McTwist	one of the most common tricks in which the rider does a back flip with a 540 (see separate glossary entry) twist
method	trick in which the front hand grabs the heel edge, both knees are bent, and the board is pulled level with the head

mute grab	move that includes gripping the right or left edge of the board with the opposite hand
powder	light, dry, fresh snow
professional	someone who does something for money rather than just for fun
run	one person's turn to perform
720	spin consisting of two full revolutions
sideslip	slide at an angle down a slope
slalom	downhill race in which competitors follow a winding course and zigzag through gates (see separate glossary entry)
stalefish	trick in which the rear hand grabs the heel edge behind the rear leg and in between the bindings while the rear leg is straight
stance	position in which someone stands on a board
straight air	trick in which a rider goes into the air and turns 180 degrees to reenter the pipe
stuck	past tense of *stick*; to make a perfect landing
terrain	ground seen in terms of its surface features

Index